THE SIMPLE LIFE

KITA SZPAK

Motivational
LEADERS IN GLOBAL PUBLISHING

Published by Motivational Press, Inc.
7777 N Wickham Rd, # 12-247
Melbourne, FL 32940
www.MotivationalPress.com

Manufactured in the United States of America.

ISBN: 978-62865-071-6

Contents

In memory of my Dad who showed me how
to live the SIMPLE life

FOREWORD:
ON WRITING THE SIMPLE LIFE

Shiny Objects Not Required

I thought for months what my next book should be about. What gnawed at me non-stop was the fact that most people's lives are so full, so jam-packed that they don't have time for themselves and for the things they really want to do. Sound like you? The premise for this book then became clear.

Our schedules are bursting at the seams. We're getting less sleep and becoming more overweight. We're held hostage by our gadgets. If we do get a spare moment, we don't know what to do with it because it's been so long since we've had a good, honest break.

How do we reverse this trend? Remember, it's taken all your life to get to where you are now so understandably it's going to take some time to undo the shackles you've chained yourself to.

This book will help you remove and avoid the myriad of shiny objects that dazzle and distract you from living a simpler but infinitely more satisfying life.

You're probably thinking this is easier said than done, and I totally agree with you. That's why I've written **The SIMPLE Life** to make it easier for you to disengage from the craziness of life without having to go into a cave to do it. This book is a solution to your problem of not having enough time to be yourself and do what makes you happy in your life.

The SIMPLE Life will not magically remove all challenges that may arise. I can't promise a problem-free life upon completing this book – no one can. However, I can assure you that once you have read it, you will have the foresight to know how to respond to the challenges that do arise and the thoughtfulness to avoid the messy situations you might otherwise find yourself in.

The SIMPLE Life contains six chapters. Each chapter has been assigned a letter in the word "SIMPLE." The letters of each chapter represent two or three key words that are essential components of living the SIMPLE life. Lucky for me, "Sleep" and "Sex" make up Chapter One. I don't know of any other two words that I could say to you that would capture your attention.

So let's get to it. In whatever format works for you, plug into **The SIMPLE Life**.

Here's to a SIMPLE life for you,

Kita *Szpak*
December 9, 2013

Chapter One: "S" - Sleep and Sex

Sleep and the SIMPLE life

I'm going to talk about sleep first because if you're not getting enough sleep, it's a good bet you're too tired to have sex. There are a number of factors why sleep deficit has become the norm. Unfortunately, sleep deprivation causes havoc during our waking hours.

Our workplace is not confined to work hours; it reaches us 24 hours a day. Thanks to smart phones and tablets, we are plugged in nonstop. With work demands spilling into what used to be our "off" hours, we've had to take time from the rest of our day to satisfy the work monster. (You can take this figuratively or literally. I leave it up to you.)

And those "off" hours haven't lightened up any. In fact, between dropping off the dry cleaning, picking up your kids from daycare, getting to the bank to discuss your mortgage, taking your son to soccer practice, and stopping off at the corner store to get batteries (again!) because you got the wrong size the first time, you've eaten up most of your daylight hours. Throw in dinner, a phone call to your mom, reviewing tomorrow's slides, and catching the last half of *The Walking Dead*. Before you know it, it's 11 p.m. and you haven't even checked e-mails yet. Once you have, you drop into bed and it's midnight. At this point you're probably feeling like a ripe pumpkin and who can blame you?

You'd think falling asleep would be easy. Unfortunately, you're so tired and also SO WIRED, making it difficult to drift off. The body may be horizontal, but the mind is running at warp speed. This internal thinking of losing control is called stress.

You are responding to the fact that the pace that you're running your life is coming dangerously close to being unsustainable. Your mind is running a mile a minute with these types of thoughts:

Did I remember to shut off heat pump?

Is it this Sunday we're supposed to go to brunch with John and Wendy?

Did I insert page numbers in the presentation? Damn, I've already sent it in for review.

I've got to go in for an oil check this week.

Oh yeah, the end of the month is my birthday. I need to have my license renewed. Where did I leave the ownership? Glove compartment, right???

Does any of this sound familiar?

It's now well past midnight. Your exhausted body and racing mind aren't doing you any favors. But there's more that's preventing you from falling asleep. That itty, bitty light coming in through the blinds - unnoticeable when you first hit the sack - now feels like a strobe light. Whether you cover your eyes with an arm or the blanket, you know it's there and it will find you. And it will win.

You're somewhat settled, but only momentarily, as another invader violates the privacy of your bedroom: the almost imperceptible sound of a leaking faucet. It may as well be a booming gong! Once detected, it will drive you crazy until you shut it off. So up you go to silence the culprit.

"Perhaps some TV will settle me down," you say to yourself at 1:15 a.m. On goes the tube that's perched on the stand at the end of your bed, flooding your room with noise and light – more stimulation for your already hyped-up system.

At some point you doze off, but you can't believe it when the Riiiiiiiiiiiiiiiiiinnnnnnnnnnnnnnnnnng of the alarm clock goes off, letting you know it's 6:30 a.m. Time to get up and go through another day, this time more tired than yesterday. Sleep deprived? Absolutely. Living the SIMPLE life? Absolutely not.

First things first. Any adjustments and changes to your way of doing things - even if the things you are doing are NOT GOOD for you - will not be easy. Habits die hard, and I'd be lying to you if I said getting to the SIMPLE life is a piece of cake. However, if you change one small thing and then another and another, you'll soon unshackle the chains.

So, back to the subject of sleep and getting more of it. Let's take a look at your bedroom. Your sleeping area has to have the following in order for you to get a good night's sleep:

- **Darkness:** If the blinds or curtains let in too much light, your body isn't getting the signal that it's time to wind down and end the day. Invest in some heavier drapes to create the darkness your body requires. Wearing a blindfold (the kind you get on overnight flights) is an equally good and less-expensive option.

- **Quiet:** Noise is a key distraction that prevents you from nodding off. It also prevents you from focusing. Short of calling in the plumber to fix that leaky faucet or the cops on your party-animal neighbor, insulate yourself from unwanted noise by shutting the bedroom door, using your blanket or pillow as a muffler, wearing ear plugs or - if worse comes to worse - moving into another room if your partner is a disruptive snorer. The latter may invite some heated discussion, but if either of you is sleep deprived, this move may be a relationship saver in the long run.

- **Comfort in Coolness:** Your body heats up during sleep so it's wise to have the temperature in the bedroom at a cool setting. An open window is also an option, but that depends on the noise levels of your neighborhood and the temperature outside.

- **Gadgets Off:** The TV is a bedroom staple these days. Watching TV before sleeping is like doing 50 pushups and then wondering why your heart is beating faster. Do yourself a favor and turn the TV, radio, iPad and iPhone off. For that matter, banish them from the bedroom altogether. It sounds extreme but good sleep requires no shiny objects.

Allison G. Harvey, a sleep specialist and psychology professor at the University of California at Berkeley, says that it takes time for people to wind down at night. The problem is that light exposure before sleep can disrupt body rhythms and suppress the release of the hormone melatonin, which promotes sleep. Hence, that TV screen is no friend of yours when it comes to getting some decent ZZZs.[1]

And if you can get rid of the alarm as well, you're on your way to the SIMPLE life. If you adjust to going to sleep naturally and waking up naturally, you'll find the ideal rhythm where your body tells you how much sleep it needs and gives you a clear signal when you should hit the sack. Having more energy as a result of sleeping well will pay off in all areas of your life – including sex.

---

1   2011 Sleep in America Poll: http://www.sleepfoundation.org/article/press-release/annual-sleep-america-poll-exploring-connections-communications-technology-use-.

Sex and the SIMPLE life

As I'm writing this, E.L. James' novel "Fifty Shades of Grey" and its two sequels have sold 95 million copies around the world.[2] There's a part of me that wonders whether I should be writing erotica instead and have my ship come in too. Yet my authentic side is nodding her head and thinking, "Shades of Shiny Objects."

Many of us wonder whether our sex lives are "normal" or "average." The need to compare our sex drive, feelings, frequency, kinkiness, number of partners, performance, places and positions – whether privately by reading a book or publicly by talking to a buddy or girlfriend - is human. We are damn curious about sex and that's a good thing. Otherwise, there wouldn't be many of us left in this world!

Sex excites, titillates and arouses, especially when it is new. The anticipation of having sex with someone new – throw in attractiveness and you almost can't stand it - is so intensely

---

2   The World's Top-Earning Authors: http://www.forbes.com/sites/jeffbercovici/2013/08/12/the-worlds-top-earning-authors-with-50-shades-e-l-james-debuts-at-no-1/

pleasurable that the act itself may in fact be anticlimactic.

Why? This is because our brain is our most important sex organ. What we think about sex is how we will play it out. The new and unknown are great mind teasers; the tried and true routine - whether it involves sex or anything else - will eventually drive our mind to boredom. Hence the sale of 95 million books to discover something new, different and exciting about sex that we haven't heard or experienced before.

There's a slight problem with this picture, though. If the tried and true eventually drives you to boredom then won't you forever be chasing after something new, different and exciting? Will it be one new, shiny object after another? Will you continually be looking for the next best thing to satisfy you? Seems like a vicious cycle to me that will expend a lot of time, energy and expense.

Positive psychology researchers - in particular professors Sonja Lyubomirsky, Ed Diener and Martin Seligman - have investigated what makes us happy.[3] The first kind of choice they looked at was the pursuit of personal pleasures, among them having sex. They discovered that this pleasure does increase our happiness, but only temporarily for a few hours or a few days at most. Not very fulfilling, is it?

Could all this be made easier living the SIMPLE life? You bet. Let's see how.

As I mentioned earlier, our brain is our most important sex organ. What we think about sex will determine what kind of significance it holds in our life. If sex is thought of as a pleasurable act of physical intimacy and nothing more, then the need for new liaisons often is likely to be the case. On the other hand, if sex is thought of as a pleasurable act of physical intimacy with someone whom we care about and love, then by extension we will also be intimate with them emotionally. The emotional bond first created

3   The Chopra Center | Week 5: Open Your Heart: http://www. chopra.com/8wk-hp-wk5-oyh

by our innermost thoughts is basic to good sex. And good sex is a key component of the SIMPLE life.

The pleasures of good sex go beyond the feel-good emotions. According to the Chopra Center, loving touch is particularly vital to health and happiness. It releases a shower of natural pain-relieving and mood-elevating chemicals throughout the body, calming the mind's busy chatter and promoting feelings of safety, comfort and relaxation. While technology allows us to see and hear each other from a distance, it can't create the true connection and fulfillment that comes from loving touch. I emphasize the word *loving* as opposed to just copping a feel.

Good sex in the SIMPLE life is based on three key factors:

- **Emotional Intimacy:** Experiencing good sex necessitates the development of emotional intimacy first. The act of sex is a natural outcome of intimacy between two people, not the cause of this intimacy.

- **Open Communication:** Talking through any issues, remaining curious and having the willingness to try out different places, positions and accessories with the partner you trust will help keep things new and unknown. Shiny objects may be looked at, but they will no longer have the substance to hold your attention for long.

- **Inner Peace:** I think make-up sex is often cited as the most satisfying type of sex there is because it occurs when mutual forgiveness and acceptance is present. Each partner is at peace having forgiven and accepted the other completely. As a healthy relationship matures, the inner peace in each partner is not just triggered in a moment of forgiveness and acceptance, but also grows to be a constant in their life together.

This inner state of peace is the essence of living the SIMPLE life, whether as a couple or as a single person. Self-forgiveness and self-acceptance will awaken your inner peace (it's always

been in you) as you uncover "me, myself and I"
– the "I" in SIMPLE in the following chapter.

Personal Notes

Chapter Two: "I" - Me, Myself and I

Me, Myself and I and the SIMPLE life

I've titled this chapter "Me, Myself and I" to clarify the meaning of "I." "I" is "you" who is reading this sentence right now. The reference to uncovering yourself found at the end of Chapter One is essential to living the SIMPLE life. You need to know what makes you tick in order to understand why you do the things you do and why you let people do the things they do to you. This looking inward is not a one-time deal. It will continue throughout your life. Taking the first step to listen to what is going on inside of you takes courage and time – and hopefully you've made some time by following the advice in the previous chapter. Knowing yourself honestly will make living the SIMPLE life a reality. Ready? Let's go …

I've always wondered why every group exercise begins with these words: There's no "I" in "team." When I first heard this expression, it grated me. How can I contribute to a team if I have to completely dispense with who I am and disown myself in order to benefit the proceedings? These questions would lead me to the next self-talk tandem where I would spend a number of minutes chastising myself for being so self-centered. Then I would question whether I even had anything worthwhile to contribute to a team. So much for group empowerment.

Interesting thought process, isn't it? The dismantling of the individual to fit into the group dynamic – to conform – whether in a team-building exercise or in a traditional family, for instance, encourages a tribe mentality where all members follow the same values, share the same opinions and do not associate with anyone or any group that does not think or act the same way. With uniformity seen as strength here, the act of taking time to think about things is discouraged. In fact, the only timeout most of us know is sending a six-year-old to his or her room for misbehaving or an imposed stoppage in play on the sports field. If you are conditioned from an early age to associate quiet time or a timeout with being punished or being interrupted, then the idea of withdrawing from the busyness of life to find quiet and be quiet is perceived as unnecessary and a negative.

Our culture's emphasis on doing – even if the action produces little or no appreciable result – is judged far more worthwhile than sitting quietly or taking a walk and doing nothing. Do you see why the SIMPLE life can be challenging to attain in our present setting of doing rather than just being? Heaven forbid that you respond to an invite with, "Thanks, but I don't really feel like going out tonight; I just want to be by myself." Wham! Just like that you've unleashed the following questions, "Are you okay? Is there something wrong? Did I say something to put you off?"

When you begin to take time to uncover yourself, you will get such reactions from family and friends – those who know you well. They may tell you you're not being yourself. The irony is that you're not. You're choosing to change your behavior to uncover the real you. The only way to do this is by retreating into quiet and taking stock.

Essentially, you're shutting out noise, distractions and shiny objects that have kept you busy – some for no real reason at all. You may come to this conclusion as you think and listen to yourself.

And where will you find a place to do your thinking – **alone** and in **silence**? Here are some suggestions:

- **Inside:** In the tub, in church, in your office behind closed doors, at the library, at the cottage, in your bedroom, on a long drive.

- **Outside:** On a walk, in the park, along the beach, your hiding place when you were a kid.

All settled? Good. Now that you've found the time and place to be with yourself, where do you begin? How do you tame a mind that's been pulled in all directions since as long as you can remember?

In Chapter Three, we'll examine the means you can use to tame the power of your mind in order to remove complications and choose the SIMPLE life.

Personal Notes

CHAPTER THREE: "M" - MIND AND MINDFULNESS

Mind and the SIMPLE life

Bear with me as I take a moment or two to distinguish between *mind* the noun and *mind* the verb. Grammar is not the sexiest of subjects, but it is necessary to understand the difference. Why? Because the two minds come into play as we explore you, your mind and the SIMPLE life.

Webster's New Encyclopedic Dictionary defines the noun *mind* as "the element or complex of elements in an individual that feels, perceives, thinks, wills and especially reasons." When *mind* is used as an action word - mind your manners or mind the stairs – it means "to pay attention to" or "be aware of." If you examine these meanings more closely, you will discover that the mind you use to think with is an internal activity whereas minding the stairs is an external action occurring because of

WHAT YOU ARE THINKING as in, "Boy, these stairs look steep; I better watch where I'm going."

An external action naturally follows the thought that has been processed in the mind moments before. How many thoughts do you think go through your mind in one day? Five hundred? Two thousand? Try thousands. That's the average number of thoughts a human brain produces daily.

No wonder you feel overwhelmed! This is especially true when you give yourself no opportunity to take time to think about things. The result is accidents, incidents, mistakes, misunderstandings and wrong decisions. Then one day you find yourself asking, "How did it ever come to this?" Have I convinced you to shut out the noise? I sure hope that's the case. You can't get to the SIMPLE life without experiencing personal quiet first.

The decision has been made. You're taking a walk to think about things. And the question is where do you start? I bet your mind is racing like a pinball as it hits the thoughts tumbling in your mind - the school play, work appointments, the stain on your shirt, the broken door handle, the light bulb that needs replacing. So much to do in such little time. Take a deep breath and concentrate on your breathing. This will help you focus on one thing rather than many.

Without disciplining your mind, it will control you with the thousand random thoughts vying for your immediate attention every day. Obviously, taking a timeout once in a while is not going to make a huge difference in the life you now have. What is needed is a regularly adhered to appointment with yourself. Whether it's a walk, a bath or a few minutes in the morning, you choose what's best for you and stick with it. The intention to still the mind will feed into the action of being quiet and force the mind to be aware of itself – "to mind" itself.

Once you get used to stilling your mind in your quiet moments, the more important questions that need addressing in your life will get the attention they deserve. This kind of reflection becomes a self-assessment based on what you believe or value. We call it your belief system. I'm not talking about religious or spiritual beliefs, although they do make up a part of the whole. You have hundreds of beliefs that you've accumulated since you first came into this world. Everything from choosing chocolate ice cream because it tastes better than vanilla to buying a Ford because dad always has to not swimming in fresh water because of snakes. The latter are relatively trivial, but if you prod deeper, more profound values and judgments will emerge such as:

People on welfare are lazy.

I don't trust lawyers.

Religion is for people who are weak.

Monogamy is impossible.

I can't do better because I don't know the right people.

Where does all this stuff come from? Family, friends, colleagues, coaches, partners, school, cultural conditioning, upbringing and life events have all contributed to what you believe. In doing a personal inventory – maybe for the first time in your adult life - you will come across things that you really like about yourself and things that embarrass you or cause you pain. It's how you respond to this personal inventory of beliefs that will determine the person you remain or grow into.

Beliefs that worked at 25 may not be useful anymore. Maybe what Mom and Dad used to say is not sitting well with you. Perhaps the remark of a new friend has caused some discomfort. Why? Carrying beliefs that you pretend to hold dear or doing things because they've always been done that way is not a reason to do so. If you become uncomfortable while uncovering yourself in quiet moments, this new awareness of mind "minding itself" is exactly what should happen in your quest for the SIMPLE life. Mind "minding itself" is "mindfulness," which we'll examine in the next section.

Mindfulness and the SIMPLE life

According to David Rock, author of "Your Brain at Work," mindfulness is the ability to be meta-cognitive or to think about your thinking. Once you become aware of your thoughts during quiet moments, you can gradually transfer this awareness into your everyday actions. When we say a person is thoughtful, we mean that person is deliberately thinking and acting for the good of himself and/or another person or situation. This premeditated behavior is actually the result of being mindful. Between the initial thought and the action there is a pause – the moment of thinking what is best in this situation. It's like stepping out of yourself to be an observer of your own behavior while still being physically present.

Dr. Jamie Gruman, Associate Professor of Organizational Behavior at the University of Guelph in Canada, has focused exclusively on this internal pause and its significance for our well-being. His research has led him to coin this quietening of the mind as "halcyonic well-being," a state of contentment that does not need any action or movement toward accomplishment or goal attainment to make a person happy.[4]

Why look at mindfulness in the context of the SIMPLE life? Isn't it rather complicated? Why can't we just leave things the way they are?

Your power to pick and choose effectively is based on your awareness of self or the ability to be mindful. Without this inner knowing, you don't have a point of reference to filter what's coming at you in life. If there's no filter between you and the world, everything comes at you at the same speed and at the same face value – whether it's a shiny new car or a heartfelt experience.

Mindfulness is a line of defense that lets you welcome the priceless and block the cheap stuff. In this way, the clutter of a shiny but superficial life is replaced with the simplicity of treasured traditions, people, possessions and way of being – what I would call the SIMPLE life.

---

4   Dr. Jamie Gruman presented the paper "Halcyonic Well-being" at the 2012 inaugural meeting of the Canadian Positive Psychology Conference in Toronto.

Personal Notes

CHAPTER FOUR: "P" - PLAN AND PLAY

Plan and the SIMPLE life

As pointed out, mindfulness gives you the power to make good decisions for yourself in the moment. It also gives you the advantage to anticipate what may be coming around the corner. It prepares you to start planning your life purposefully. How? Once your level of awareness has been raised, the likelihood of dropping back into a busy, scheduled life without questioning it is like watching a bathtub overflowing and wondering why the floor is wet.

With personal awareness, you cannot help but see and feel things more clearly. If your issues are challenging, you may deliberately mask such painful realizations with drugs, alcohol, compulsive shopping, eating, gaming, etc. Unfortunately, life's shiny objects are not just playful and distracting; some of them can be deadly too.

While mindfulness gives you the power to make good decisions, other factors in your life may require third party support and counseling. Having the courage to seek help is a manifestation of mindfulness as is reading this book. Though one is an extreme measure, both initiatives represent positive action on your part – a good step forward.

It's highly unlikely for you to take off and avoid life's bumps, although this thought has probably entered your mind from time to time. That would be too simple. Perhaps you can be like the rabbit that stands very still hoping not to be seen in broad daylight. By standing still and doing nothing, you elude life and its challenges. Recent discussion on authentic happiness identifies "engagement" and "meaning and purpose" as two of five measureable elements contributing to one's overall well-being.

You can be the most mindful person in the world who does nothing or the most mindful person in the world who does something. Both kinds of people exist. Those doing something about it have purpose whereas those doing nothing – even with the discipline of quietening their mind - may lack meaning in their life. Putting happiness aside, if you are mindful with purpose then you will plan and move your life forward.

By combining your now-robust belief system with your passion – that which you like to do and probably do well - you create purpose. Having meaning in your life drives you. This internal engine makes planning easier because goal setting is defined by what you want to accomplish. One feeds into the other fluidly without confusion or distraction and is symptomatic of the SIMPLE life.

Planning is deliberate thoughtfulness whereby a series of premeditated steps bring about a desired outcome. Notice the emotions you experience when planning: hope, resolve, optimism, excitement, and perhaps fear. This fear is generally overridden by delicious anticipation. These are positive emotions in your internal engine that drive you to action. The action that comes out of planning is creating. When these moments of creativity occur in a natural, smooth sequence without resistance, you are living a life with purpose.

Play and the SIMPLE life

There is one question that is bound to arise: Where's the spontaneity in all this? It sounds as if a purposeful life is mighty boring, too. But here's where a little play in your life balances the equation.

Who can forget the discovery of the reams of paper with the words "all work and no play makes Jack a dull boy" written repeatedly by another Jack in the 1980 movie "The Shining"? These words first appeared in 1659 in James Howell's "Proverbs in English, Italian, French and Spanish." It seems play is important to us and has been for the last 350 years. Where planning is structured, play is unstructured - its sweet gift to us.

Play creates a sense of escape. Playing is carefree, unrestricted, happy and spontaneous where rules exist that can be easily broken or done away with when they don't suit the circumstances. Above all, playing is associated with children. It may be that the innocence and naiveté of kids is what makes play their domain more than ours. The truth is there's nothing wrong with reclaiming a bit of innocence and naiveté in your life.

Has someone ever asked you to play with them? I'm referring to your adult friends and family. Has someone ever told you that they need to play more? Did you react with surprise, embarrassment, discomfort or delight? Maybe it was you who wanted to play – who still wants to play but hasn't found anyone to play with yet.

We're very good at working nonstop if need be but not very good at playing. In fact, you may feel downright guilty about taking time off because you identify your value with work so strongly that the idea of not working and not being productive makes you feel value-less. Yet to prevent yourself from being dull like Jack or burned out, play is vital to keep you balanced and centered. Light and easy has to counter heavy and hard in your life or you will feel pretty grim.

If you haven't already, I challenge you to ask someone to play with you. Their response will be an indicator if they're someone you want to have around. This is especially true if you're getting serious about wanting the SIMPLE life.

Personal Notes

CHAPTER FIVE: "L" - LOOK, LAUGH AND LOVE

Look and the SIMPLE life

Look is a word that is underestimated. Because it's used frequently every day, the word has worn out its welcome. "Take a look at this." "Look here." "Look out." "You look tired." The list of phrases goes on. If someone says, "That looks great", do they really mean it? Do you even pay attention enough to agree or disagree with them? There's no judgment here. This is just an observation about the word and what significance it actually carries in a life that is lived simply and vitally.

If you've learned to be mindful with your thoughts, it's probable that you will take this thoughtfulness externally to your senses, too. As far as the sense of sight, you can become mindful with your eyes. This, of course, extends to hearing, touch and taste as well. But for our purposes, we'll focus on the sense of sight and looking with mindfulness – excuse the pun.

Have you ever gone for a walk on a neighborhood street and noticed something out of the ordinary, such as a rabbit or raccoon? The operative word here is *noticed* as there is nothing to look at if nothing is noticed in the first place. Noticing demands attention from you. It demands your awareness of things around you. Once you are aware of them, you can respond by looking at them.

It's straightforward, isn't it? But few people actually see and take in their surroundings. Your preoccupation with thousands of random thoughts may cause you to miss a lot of what's going on around you. Add a smart phone and chances are you're seeing nothing in your midst. The disconnect is total, making this scenario the perfect setup for incidents, accidents, confusion and most importantly, missed opportunities. Research conducted by Harvard University psychologists Daniel Gilbert and Mathew Killingsworth concluded that 46.9 percent of the time people are doing what's called "mind wandering" - looking into their own thoughts and not focusing on the outside world or the task at hand.

Not seeing the cute bunny is minor, but not realizing the guy who just bumped you is the marketing executive you've wanted to meet for the last six months is a bigger deal. Life presents nuggets of opportunities when you least expect it. If you're not looking, you're missing out. Do yourself a favor and become mindful with your eyes. They'll show you life's jewels right there in front of you.

Laugh and the SIMPLE life

We talked about play and its characteristics in the last chapter. It's not difficult to make the connection between playing and laughing. Where one is the other follows because both are activators rather than inhibitors. Have you ever tried to stop laughing? Have you ever ended a golf game because it was too much fun? Thankfully, the limit for too much laughter is limitless, unless you're sitting in Mr. Appleby's history class. Or you may have been lucky and had a teacher who was funny. You probably remember more from that class than any other. Laughing while you learn can be an effective way to retain information; there is certainly no stress in the process. There are many health benefits to laughter, such as the reduction of the stress hormones cortisol, epinephrine, adrenaline, dopamine and growth hormone. It also increases the level of health-enhancing hormones, such as endorphins. It even creates a stronger immune system by increasing the number of antibody-producing cells and enhancing the effectiveness of T cells.[5] And yes, I wish I was a comedian making you split your sides while you continue reading.

Is there a downside to laughing? I've not found one other than getting kicked out of class or popping stitches after abdominal surgery. Turns out the laughter yoga class was just too much. And yes, there really are laughter yoga classes out there.

---

5   The Stress Management and Health Benefits of Laughter: http://stress.about.com/od/stresshealth/a/laughter.htm

Love and the SIMPLE life

To even begin writing about love causes me to pause mightily. Where do I start? Let me count the ways. All of these words are associated with love: emotion, feeling, risk, chemistry, caring, sex, agitated pheromones, loss, vulnerability, poetry, attraction, soul mate, lust, agape, meeting of minds, broken heart, bliss, affection, etc. The list goes on depending on what you've experienced or are experiencing now. Love is uniquely subjective. It is in the eyes of the beholder. You cannot possibly know what another human being experiences of love. For this reason, not only are you blind when in love, but you're also blind to another's experience of this powerful force.

Before we go any further, this emotion is not just confined to loving another human being. You can have great love for a pet, job, song, story or place that evokes a profoundly deep and caring response from you. If you take this line of thinking further, the more touch points in your life that elicit this kind of reaction, the richer and fuller your life is.

Are there companion pieces to love in the SIMPLE life that make it fuller, that give it a richness that can take your breath away? I'd like to posit three elements here that might just do that. They are wisdom, clarity and compassion.

We associate wisdom with old age but having wisdom is not so much about being old as it is about applying the knowledge and understanding to your own life. Wisdom is not the accumulation of information. It is a thoughtful interpretation and application of information that enables you to respond to life and its challenges with love.

Wisdom's seeing companion is clarity, which is the ability and courage to look clearly at a situation and grasp all aspects before making a decision to act. Where there is drama mixed with shiny objects, clarity is absent. In the jangle of smoke and mirrors, your vision is obstructed until a life-changing event lifts the superficial veil and you see clearly. It is only then that clarity allows you to glimpse into the SIMPLE life, perhaps for the very first time.

Wisdom's feeling companion is compassion, which is an immensely profound emotion that gifts you with the power to feel for another human being. This stepping outside of self brings you full circle from first retreating within to gradually extending outward in body and spirit. Having compassion for others is a characteristic of those who understand the benefits of living the SIMPLE life.

I'd like to leave you with a final image that will best enforce these companion elements that are so important in your life. Have you heard of the four horsemen of the Apocalypse? Although some interpretations differ, the four riders are commonly seen as symbolizing Pestilence, War, Famine and Death. Well, I'd like to call forth four other horsemen, those of earthly revelation representing wisdom, clarity, compassion and love. Let them lead you to look, laugh and love more in your life.

Personal Notes

Chapter Six: "E" - Eat and Exercise

Eat and the SIMPLE life

In Chapter One, we began with externals sleep and sex and we are ending this book with two other significant externals – "eat" and "exercise." Having a healthy approach to food is the best way to enjoy it. Because eating keeps you alive, the idea of containing or controlling it by eliminating or treating it like the enemy is contrary to living a naturally SIMPLE life.

There will always be diets and fads that promise weight loss and a new, improved you. These come and go. Like shiny objects, they attract you. You try them, and maybe for a little while you reach your objective. But when your metabolism slows to starvation mode, you indulge and gain back the weight and then some. Back on the diet you go, repeating the pattern much to your dismay, debilitating you physically and psychologically.

Hopefully the information in the previous chapters has already helped you form a context for what, how and why you eat. No energy? Getting too little sleep? Sweets may be what you reach for. Eat at the counter or in the car because you have no time to sit down and enjoy a meal? Fast food is the ticket for a jam-packed life where taking time to eat slowly is unheard of. Bored? Eating fills your stomach and your time just like TV when you allow these buddies in the same room. The two are deadly together.

Emotionally spent? Craving love and care? Sometimes you eat to fill the hole you have in your heart and soul, making the pain subside. It is a form of self-medication. Of course, you and I know that food is not the solution for the emptiness you are feeling. It's just a temporary distraction.

You need to take the following steps to develop a healthy approach to eating: initial awareness, introspection, mindfulness, self-acceptance, thoughtful planning and execution. Remember, it took you a while to get where you are today. Be patient as you establish a positive relationship with food. Dispense with the shiny objects of quick fixes and dedicate yourself to fundamental habits that will enable you to eat to live the SIMPLE life. One of these essentials is exercise, which we will examine next.

Exercise and the SIMPLE life

Research has shown that exercise can lead to a better brain.[6] That statement should drive us all to exercising frantically, but this is not the case. My son taught me an important lesson that I've never forgotten about exercising a number of years ago. He was eleven at the time and very much his father's son; both loved to read. Although I am fond of books, I'll choose an outdoor run over a good read any day. In any case, I was determined to get my oldest boy outside and moving as much as possible (or rather as much as I was). It was during one of these encouraging jags of mine where I asked my son to go to the park or for a hike that he

6   How Exercise Can Lead to a Better Brain: http://www.ny-times.com/2012/04/22/magazine/how-exercise-could-lead-to-a-better-brain.html?pagewanted=all

turned to me and said in a pleading tone, "Mom, I'm not like you; I never will be."

Well, you could have hit me with a ton of bricks and I would not have felt as much pain as I did when I heard those words. He was not me, and I had no right to think that he would enjoy the same things I did. In this case, he wasn't keen on hiking, moving, running or getting out like I was. Exercise was not a joy to him; it was more like a chore.

Because of this personal experience, I am keenly aware of how hard it must be to exercise when you are not motivated to do so. When you don't like something, it's tougher to do it. The motivation has to come from somewhere. It's here that your mindfulness steps in to assist you in establishing the reasons you should exercise. These reasons can range from health concerns, a desire to lose weight, being able to play with your children, boosting energy and improving your sex drive. When you set parameters, you're the boss. Emotion takes a back seat to the personal responsibility you've set in place to improve your life by exercising.

Such a decision is empowering and is characteristic of the self-empowerment that happens when you embark upon the SIMPLE life. This is not a diet but a quality-of-life change that will free you from calorie counting to counting the good things in your life.

Personal Notes

Closing Thoughts: "C" + "T" = Care and Trust

Closing thoughts can be tricky. I could get weepy and thank you profusely for reading my book. But that's not me. And it's certainly not the type of reader you are. You don't need someone hanging on your arm, tugging at it and looking for approval. What I will say is that I care that you have read this book, and I trust that you will take from it what you want and need to make your life simpler.

Here's a cautionary tale. In the months that I was writing **The SIMPLE Life**, "Imagine" author Jonah Lehrer had his life unravel at lightning speed. A persistent reporter uncovered that he had borrowed content from earlier blogs and made up supposedly unearthed Bob Dylan quotes found in "Imagine." His book was removed from retail shelves and will no longer be printed. He was dropped by his publishers and resigned from his job. Ironically, Lehrer was later paid to talk about his lies and deceptions.[7]

---

7   Jonah Lehrer: I 'Plagiarized,' 'Lied,' 'Caused Deep Pain'; Is Paid $20,000 To Discuss Misdeeds: http://www.huffingtonpost.com/2013/02/12/jonah-lehrer-knight-plagiarized-lied_n_2671140.html?utm_hp_ref=books&ir=Books-

But here's the real twist that makes life unpredictably worthwhile: Simon and Shuster struck a deal with Lehrer to write "A Book About Love," expected for release at the end of 2014.[8] Has Lehrer discovered the SIMPLE life? I hope he has, and I hope that you have too. Truth be told, I've got my money on you.

Take good care,
Kita

---

8   A Fallen New Yorker Writer Signs With Simon & Schuster: http://www.nytimes.com/2013/06/07/business/media/after-his-fall-jonah-lehrer-shops-a-book-on-the-power-of-love.html?_r=0

CPSIA information can be obtained at www.ICGtesting.com
Printed in the USA
LVOW05s2316180414

382340LV00005B/16/P